William P. (William Parsons) Atkinson

The Study of Politics

An Introductory Lecture

William P. (William Parsons) Atkinson

The Study of Politics
An Introductory Lecture

ISBN/EAN: 9783337072650

Printed in Europe, USA, Canada, Australia, Japan

Cover: Foto ©Suzi / pixelio.de

More available books at **www.hansebooks.com**

THE

STUDY OF POLITICS

An Introductory Lecture

BY

WILLIAM P. ATKINSON

PROFESSOR OF ENGLISH AND HISTORY IN THE MASSACHUSETTS
INSTITUTE OF TECHNOLOGY

BOSTON
ROBERTS BROTHERS
1888

NOTE.

THE following Lecture grew out of an introduction to a course on Constitutional History given to the Senior Class at the Institute of Technology, and has been read at that admirable institution, the Boston Young Men's Christian Union, and elsewhere. In now printing it, the writer desires to be alone held responsible for the opinions it contains.

THE STUDY OF POLITICS.

THAT learned historian Professor Freeman has gone so far as to say that " History is only past politics, politics only present history." The statement has perhaps as much truth in it as such epigrammatic statements usually have; but it would be just as true to say that history is past religion, and religion is present history, or history is past political economy, or past art, or past science, — for all these come within a true and broad view of the scope of history. If, indeed, for the word " politics " the word " sociology " were to be substituted, the statement would be true enough; but that is a word which I suppose nothing could possibly induce Professor Freeman to use, and it cannot be denied that his version is true of history as commonly written. History as commonly written is too exclusively the story of the rise and fall of governments, of political struggle and political revolution; so that the genuine student of the subject will miss

the profit of the greater part of his historical reading who does not come to it prepared with some
general knowledge of the theory of political science.
It is as if he tried to pursue his engineering studies
without having first mastered the calculus.

It is not, however, because the science of politics
is one main key to the study of the history of the
past that I want to fix your attention upon it to-
day.   It has a stronger practical claim than that.
The study of politics is a young man's necessary
preparation for the intelligent performance of his
duties as a citizen and a voter; it is a young
woman's necessary preparation for contributing
her share to the formation of an intelligent public
opinion, to the doing of her duty as sister, as
mother, as wife, and as friend, to help, and even
to constrain, if need be, the masculine voter to
keep always in the path of patriotism and duty.
Now, is it not a little strange that an idea should
be so prevalent among men who boast of being
" practical " that however it may be with other
kinds of knowledge, political knowledge is of a
kind that comes by nature or by instinct or by
reading newspapers?   It is not always the politicians of the corner-groceries, — who are also
" practical," — but often men who should know

better, who are fond of calling students of the subject " literary fellows " and " kid-glove politicians ; " and we all know, for we in Massachusetts have had excellent opportunity for observing, how impudent and unscrupulous demagogues can trade in this way on the ignorance and prejudices of voters. But I think that a change is fast being forced upon us in respect to this matter of political education which is quite parallel with the change that is coming over the subject of scientific education. While the country was small and the people few in number, it may be admitted that their general intelligence could pretty safely be depended on for the proper guidance of public affairs, — just as while our buildings were small they were built by carpenters who had small pretensions to architectural knowledge, or when our roads were simple, the farmers worked out their own road-tax, while their wives and daughters plied the spinning-wheel or wove the homespun. But it takes something more than the carpenter's rule-of-thumb to erect the vast structures of to-day. The village mechanic could build the old village meeting-house; but it requires an architect, and a good one, to build Trinity yonder. The farmers cannot turn out with pick and shovel to build a railroad, — that takes an engineer; while nobody but that crack-brained man of genius Mr. Ruskin makes any attempt nowadays to restore the spinning-wheel, or thinks of railing at a cotton-mill.

Precisely such a change has come over us in respect to politics. They can no longer be conducted by rule-of-thumb; our political interests are too vast, our unprincipled demagogues too numerous and too dangerous. It took our fathers comparatively little trouble to find out Washington and place him at the head of affairs, to find out Adams and Hamilton and Madison and Marshall. They had not so many good men to pick from, nor so many rogues to fear. It takes all that honest men can do to put competent men into office nowadays, and too often the problem is too much for them. How can the hands of honest men be strengthened? I know of but one sure way, and that is by the spread of sound political knowledge. Suppose that each one of you were to resolve that as far as in him lay he would learn to know his duties as a citizen as well as he means to know his business as a chemist, an architect, or an engineer, — to know his duties, and to have ideas and to stand by them, — you would not fail to find yourselves, through the possession of such knowl-

edge and such independence, in a position of
commanding influence in whatever circle you
might move; for, as Stuart Mill well says, "One
man with a conviction is stronger than ten who
have only interests." At the meeting in Boston
at the opening of the last Presidential campaign
called to protest against the discreditable Republican nomination for President, I could not but
admire the position of the man who made the chief
speech of the occasion. He was not a professional
politician, he was a clergyman; but one who thinks
it a part of his clerical duty openly and on all
occasions to take what he conceives to be the side
of truth and honesty and righteousness in politics.
It was cheering to observe the weight which his
simple words carried with them, coming as they
did from a man whom everybody respected, and
who throughout his long life has never been wanting in the courage of his convictions, though he
has never sought political distinction.[1] It was the
case of an honest and fearless man coming simply
forward to do his political duty at a moment when
he was privileged to exercise a great influence,
because the words of honest and fearless men were
greatly needed. But it is the influence which each

[1] Rev. James F. Clarke, D.D.

one of us is bound to exercise all through his life, whether his influence be a great or a small one; and we cannot exert it rightly without political knowledge.

You will perceive at once that I am myself a "mugwump." Let me say here at the very outset that in this lecture and in those that will follow I purpose to express my own honest convictions in as plain and forcible a manner as my command of the English language will allow; and I shall do this whether my illustrations shall chance to be drawn from questions long since settled, or from the political issues of the day. But I need not say to you who know me that in no case shall I do it in order that I may make you proselytes to my own opinions, but that I may teach you, by example as well as precept, to practise the duty and to exercise the right of speaking and thinking independently yourselves.

I say, then, that it is every man's duty to study politics, — yes, and every woman's too; "to go into politics," — though that phrase, I know, has a very bad sound, — to go over head and ears into politics. And yet I am quite aware that very honest men take a different view. "I don't care for politics," I hear some one say, "and I don't intend to meddle with them; I leave them to the politicians. I shall be too busy with honest work. Politics are a dirty business at best, infested with rogues and rascals;" and the statement is lamentably true.

Now, it cannot be denied that honest men take this ground. I have known good men who made it a boast that they had never cast a vote in all their lives; and many a man who does vote thinks it a very meritorious sacrifice to interrupt his private business in order to go to the polls. And I could not have a better illustration of the importance of right ideas in politics; for such men, whether consciously or not, are acting upon a false political theory, one that is as mischievous as it is widespread, though they probably have never taken the trouble to state it in so many words. Formulated in words, it would be something like this: Society is made up of independent individuals, each one of whom is free to act as he pleases, provided he takes care not to infringe on the right of everybody else to do the same; what we call " government " is only a sort of street constable to prevent such infringements, — a necessary nuisance; and the less of it we have, the better. So long as it goes reasonably well, a quiet man had better let it alone and attend to his own affairs. It is full of inevitable abuses; but unless they grow intolerable, he is not called upon to interfere.

Now, you see this is a theory of politics, a political philosophy, — though, as I shall try to show, a very wrong one; and the result is to belittle the subject in the minds of those who hold it. The independence of the individual being the all-important point, it is of much less consequence, such men think, in what way the individuals combine together. One form may have certain advantages over another, but on the whole, Pope's lines express the true philosophy of the matter: —

> " For forms of government let fools contest;
>   Whate'er is best administered is best."

The main point is the efficient constable: " Let the fools struggle to be made Presidents and Governors and Congressmen, I," says such a man, "have more serious work on hand. I will attend to my business and leave them to squabble for place, even if they do plunder me by taxation. If that goes too far, I suppose I must help ' turn the rascals out.'"

I am afraid this is the working political theory of many a respectable man who would be surprised to be told that it is the product of a false political philosophy. He would probably disclaim having any philosophy; nevertheless he is acting upon a theory, and one which starts with a false premise. His doctrine begins with the supposition that the political unit of calculation is the individual. There will be plenty to say before we get through about the liberty of the individual and the famous doctrine of the rights of man; but in my judgment the liberty of the individual is *not* the starting-point of political speculation, and to show that the man who, on such grounds as I have described, declines to meddle with politics is neglecting one of the greatest of life's duties, I have only to contrast this view with a truer one.

It would be much nearer the truth to say that, politically speaking, the individual standing by himself, instead of being the unit of political calculation, is nothing, is zero. To be convinced of this, try in imagination to strip yourselves of all that part of you which has been created and developed by your surroundings, and see how little is left. To begin with, you came into existence not alone in a wilderness, but are the offspring of parents and surrounded by relatives who in like manner had been born into an already organized society and formed a part of a larger collection of human

beings, — a village, a State, a nation. Thus we are
born right into a whole network of *relations* to men
and things and institutions, involving duties to all
sorts of people and surroundings; and it is almost
entirely because these people and surroundings were
what they were that you are what you are. Suppose that instead of being born, say in a New England city, you had been born in a Turcoman tent
or a Hottentot kraal: it is obvious that instead
of growing up a certain sort of New Englander,
better or worse, you would have grown up a certain sort of Turcoman or Hottentot, better or
worse; and instead of studying the calculus at the
Institute of Technology, you would now be riding
a horse and hurling a spear with the Turcomans,
or grubbing for worms for your dinner with the
Hottentots. If men, instead of coming into existence together, should come into existence absolutely isolated and alone, they are such a feeble
folk that they would all instantly perish.

This boasted individuality, therefore, appears
from this point of view to be an illusion. Instead
of society being made up of a collection of independent self-sufficing units, it turns out to be
composed of, so to speak, nothing but individual
bundles of relations, whose very individuality itself

is dependent on these relations to surrounding individuals. It is idle to talk of taking ourselves out of these relations; they make us what we are. Strip us of them, and we are nothing. We realize our true individuality only to the degree that we recognize these relations to others and perform their accompanying duties. One might as well talk of jumping off his shadow, or out of his skin, as of getting rid of them.[1]

The theoretical error, therefore, of our friend who is unwilling to meddle with politics is obvious. He is setting up for himself and trying to live alone; he might just as well try to go up in a balloon. It is as though he were to say, "I don't meddle with eating. Eating is a very troublesome business, and involves a deal of dirty work. I will have nothing to do with it; I am too busy." But we know that in this case certain physiological consequences soon begin to appear. Our abstemious friend's person would be attenuated; his

[1] A man cannot be truly called a citizen of a State or of the world unless he feels himself included in this unbroken chain of the temporal development of humanity, endowed with innumerable benefits won for him by past generations, and hence bound body and soul to the historical whole, without which his whole existence would be unthinkable, and whose unfinished work he is called upon to develop further by his own activity and intelligence. — *Lotze, Microcosmus, Eng. tr.,* vol. i. p. 100.

bodily strength would diminish; and pretty soon, if he did not take a little time from his business and devote it to his dinner, his business and he would part company forever. Well, many a man who is not so foolish as to starve his body is quite ready to starve the State, not seeing that he is equally, and even in a higher sense, dependent on its health for his own prosperity. He is willing to ignore the most important of those relations to others which make him what he is, — at least he is willing to try to reap all the advantages those relations bring him, — at the same time that he neglects all the duties they impose. If his doctrine is true for him, it is true for others; and if everybody followed it, society would perish, the State would starve. Nothing is clearer than that if a man is pretty much what his relations to others make him, those relations impose on him duties exactly commensurate with his privileges. The man who neglects his political duties is as much a moral suicide as he would be physically a suicide if he starved himself.

This subordination of the individual to society, his dependence on it for the development of all that he really is, might be illustrated by your position as students of physical science. What is it to

be a student of science? Is it to start out each on
an independent course to make new scientific dis-
coveries, and in that sense to be individual? You
very well know that individuality of that sort would
go but very little way. Instead of that, you find
yourselves set down to the task of mastering, to
the best of your ability, a great body of already
discovered and organized scientific knowledge.
You have got to make yourselves members of the
scientific body, citizens, so to speak, of the scientific State, by mastering that knowledge, not by
starting out alone to see what you can discover
for yourselves. You must patiently traverse the
whole length of the great highways of knowledge
already opened before you can reach that unknown
region where there is any chance of your being
discoverers. And the scientific college stands in
the same relation to you as a scientific student in
which the State stands to you as a citizen; only by
obediently availing yourself to the utmost of all its
opportunities can you hope to get any personal
and individual advantage. And what is a scientific
college but the representative, in its libraries and
laboratories and text-books and professors, of the
accumulated scientific knowledge of the past,
slowly organized into a form in which it can be

communicated to you? From Euclid and Aristotle, down through generation after generation of seekers after scientific truth, through Galileo and Newton, through Lyell and Faraday and Cuvier and Darwin and thousands of lesser men exploring Nature in every direction, the great world of scientific knowledge has for generations been in process of discovery and organization; and it is through these doors that you are trying to get admission, and become, as it were, citizens of this world. But it cannot be done by wilfully isolating yourself, or wilfully taking your own course; but by obediently following that beaten path which the experience of the past has marked out for you. You might conceivably take up geometry after your own fashion and rediscover all the propositions of Euclid. Something like that was done once by a youth who had never heard of Euclid. The binomial theorem has been rediscovered; you might perhaps reinvent the calculus. But what would be the use? Why leap fences and ditches when there is a highroad to travel? On the other hand, if you do not diligently travel that, you will never come to your journey's end. A well-known self-educated inventor,[1] who had originated some really ingenious

1 The late S. P. Ruggles.

machines, told me once that he should have been saved months and years of useless labor if he could have had access to an Institute of Technology when as a young man he was blindly groping his way to the valuable inventions he at last succeeded in perfecting.

And when you have come to the end of your scientific training, what is it you have accomplished but the establishing of a new set of *relations*, internal and external, — internal relations with the world of scientific thought and scientific knowledge, and, consequent on these, new external relations with the world of life and action? I leave out of view for the present the internal mental and moral change of some sort that has been going on all the time; I want you to look at the changed external relations that have been brought about by the acquisition of all this new knowledge and these new capacities which have made you different beings from what you were. You have come in contact with the world of knowledge at a great many new points, and thus indefinitely enlarged your field of action; and you have done it, not by asserting your independence and living in the woods, but by multiplying your connections. If liberty were really getting free of relations to others, you have

all this time been making yourselves slaves; but
in reality you enlarge your freedom by the addition of every new relation you form through your
new knowledge and new capacity.

Let me give a concrete illustration of what I
mean. There was here some years ago a young
man, the son of a friend of mine who was a grocer
in a country village; and when I first knew him,
the son was driving the wagon and tending store.
I persuaded his father to send him here; and he is
now, through the scientific knowledge he acquired
here, in a very responsible position in a large
manufacturing establishment. If he had stayed at
home he would probably have still been driving
his father's wagon, and in course of time would perhaps have inherited his father's business. I do not
say that that would have been a bad thing. It is
an honest business, and would probably have given
him a good living. I do not say that it was better
for him to come here simply because he is probably earning more money than he could have
earned if he had stayed at home. I do not put it
on that ground. But I think it was better for him
to come here, because by coming here he became
more of a man, because his sphere of action was enlarged, and his mental vision indefinitely extended.

He can thus put more life and a higher kind of life into a day or a year than he possibly could have done as a village grocer. But this wider sphere, and the greater freedom that goes with it, is gained by increasing, not by diminishing, the number and complexity of his relations to others.

Now, what is true in education is just as true in politics. The freest man is not the red Indian in the woods, but the man most closely involved in the network of the most complex society. The doctrine of Rousseau is the negation of all true political science. The civilized man is the only freeman; and he is free just in proportion as he is civilized. Which is freer to lead the true life of a human being, — a citizen of Boston, surrounded by the accumulated results of two centuries of progress, schools, colleges, libraries, museums, art-galleries, a city which is, as it were, a great house full of luxuries and conveniences, and furnishing opportunity for the most diversified activities; or the isolated squatter in the Western backwoods, deprived of all these? And yet here he is bound on every hand by governmental restraint. Does he enlarge his real freedom by retiring to the forest?

I met a humorous friend the other day who seemed much disturbed in his mind. "They call this a free country," he said; " but I shall have to move. I can't even kill my own cat. I put her in a bag, and was proceeding to drown her in the pond, when a policeman met me, and declared it was against the law to throw cats into the pond. I took her home again, and was proceeding to shoot her in my back-yard, when another police-man interfered, and declared it was against the law to shoot cats in back-yards. So I went to the apothecary's to buy some poison; but the apoth-ecary, eying me sternly, inquired if I had a phy-sician's prescription authorizing him to sell me poison. I assured him that I was contemplating neither homicide nor suicide, but only felicide. But it would not do; I shall have to keep that cat. And you call this a land of freedom!" But my friend is really a good citizen, and knows very well that the highest civilization brings with it the necessity for the greatest amount and greatest complexity of governmental restraint. And of all political theo-ries, that is the most false which starts with the assumption that government is a necessary evil, to be reduced to its lowest terms.[1]

1 This view, that the only business of Law is to prevent interfer-ence with the liberty of the individual, has gained undue favor on account of the real reforms to which it has led. The laws which it has helped to get rid of were really mischievous, but mischiev-

But the more complex the organization, the more numerous the duties and responsibilities it brings with it. If everybody performed all his duties, society would be perfect; if everybody neglected them, society would go all to pieces. In point of fact, society goes well or ill according as the number of those who perform all their social duties is greater or less than the number of those who neglect them. And as there is in every community an element of rascality which represents the disease of the body politic, honest and patriotic men not only have to do their fair share of political duty, but have the added labor of constant war-

ous for further reasons than those conceived by the supporters of the theory. Having done its work, the theory now tends to become obstructive, because, in fact, advancing civilization brings with it more and more interference with the liberty of the individual to do as he likes, and this theory affords a reason for resisting all positive reforms, all reforms which involve an action of the State in the way of promoting conditions favorable to moral life. It is one thing to say that the State in promoting these conditions must take care not to defeat its true end by narrowing the region within which the spontaneity and disinterestedness of true morality can have play; another thing to say that it has no moral end to serve at all, and that it goes beyond its province when it seeks to do more than secure the individual from violent interference by other individuals. — *Prof. T. H. Green, Principles of Political Obligation, Works,* vol. ii. p. 345.

See also Huxley's critique of Herbert Spencer in his Essay entitled " Administrative Nihilism."

fare with rogues and incapables, in order to prevent
society from perishing, as it inevitably does when
the rogues and incapables get the upper hand.
Hence the absolute necessity to the safety of the
State of multiplying the number of honest and
energetic men and women; and as honesty and
energy are of little avail without knowledge, there
comes the still greater necessity of educating honest men and women in political knowledge. I do
not think it is because the bulk of our voters
are politically dishonest that they are led by the
nose by plausible demagogues, it is because they
are politically ignorant. The knavish demagogue
sinks into obscurity as soon as he is found out, as
may be seen by the example of more than one
American "statesman" now living in modest re-
tirement. The difficulty is that there is constantly
a new crop of them, with new sets of political
quackeries and swindles. The only remedy for
political as for medical quackery is better education.

But let us return to our friend who minds his
own business and does not meddle with politics.
He may still urge that there are plenty of men in
the community who are fond of politics, and go
into them because they like them. Why cannot
he, he asks, a quiet man who does not like them,

leave politics to them? And of course if going into politics means going in for office, — which is all the idea many men have of going into politics, — we do not want to disturb our quiet man unless the country should absolutely require his services. But to know whether we can dispense with him, we must examine a little into the character of these men to whom he is so willing to leave the affairs of the community, — the men who are said to be fond of politics, and who enter political life because they like it. They may easily be classified. There is first the army of office-seekers, — the men who care little for the country, but much for the loaves and fishes. If they get them, they will perhaps be reasonably honest, at least so long as there is no danger of being found out; but their interest in public affairs is merely personal and selfish. They are blind adherents of the party that put them in so long as the party is triumphant; they are per-fectly willing to go over to the other side if they can get a chance when the party is defeated. I knew such a man once. When we were young he was at first a warm Abolitionist; but Abolitionism did not pay in those days, — its only pay was in kicks and curses. So he went over to the Pro-slavery Democrats, who were then in power; and as he was an effective stump-orator, — that is to say, he had a gift of saying nothing in a great many sonorous and imposing words, — his apostasy was rewarded by the gift of a fat office, for which he was entirely unfit, and which he held for many years. When the war came, and his party was overwhelmingly defeated, he had just time to jump on to the Republican car and come out a flaming patriot, —he who had been for years a servile tool of the slaveholders! And in that character he took the stump, and his gift of empty talk, which he has in unlimited measure, again secured him an unimportant place with a large salary; for having no talent but that of wirepulling and " orating," he could never rise to a position of any real importance. He has just been turned out; for this time he did not jump quick enough, — and indeed President Cleveland would have had no use for such a man, — and he has probably retired for good to the shades of private life. But not, you see, without having made a pretty good thing of politics; for he has been for many years in receipt of a large salary, now from one party, now from the other, nominally for public service, really for being what is sometimes called a "worker; " that is to say, a servile party tool.

Now, I think it is pretty clear that it would not be safe for our quiet man to leave political affairs in the hands of this class of men who are fond of politics, and go into them because they like them. They are the tools of profligate factions, the baser elements and instruments of "rings." And yet their name is legion; they are the great danger of republican institutions.

But it will be contended that there is a much higher class than this, a class who seek in politics an adequate field for really great abilities; a class who are actuated, not by love of money or of money's worth, but by love of power. These men enter the political arena because in it they see room for the satisfaction of that ambition which Milton calls the "last infirmity of noble mind," — the ambition to rule, and the fame and glory it brings with it. And when this ambition is coupled with unbending integrity and lofty patriotism it may indeed make a great hero and a great man. But when these great abilities are *not* combined with a patriotism and an integrity as great, you get the most dangerous of men, men who may indeed be instruments of much good service, services great in proportion to their great abilities, but who can never be depended on in times of trial. Such a man was Daniel Webster, a man gifted by Providence with marvellous intellectual abilities, one of the greatest brains I suppose that this country ever produced; a man who in his prime did the nation great service as the interpreter and defender of the true meaning of the Constitution; but a man who failed us in the day of trial because his motives were not pure. His ambition was not to serve his country at any personal sacrifice: his highest ambition was to be made President; and the slaveholders had only to dangle the glittering bait before his eyes to induce him to be false to the cause of freedom, and so his great light went out in darkness. The personal vices of the man had degraded the statesman, for they were such as were inconsistent with patriotism or with individual independence.

Thus sadly wrote our noble old Quaker poet of our "lost leader:" —

> "Revile him not, — the Tempter hath
>   A snare for all;
> And pitying tears, not scorn and wrath,
>   Befit his fall!
>
> "Oh! dumb be passion's stormy rage,
>   When he who might
> Have lighted up and led his age,
>   Falls back in night.
>   .   .   .   .   .   .

"Of all we loved and honored, naught
  Save power remains, —
A fallen angel's pride of thought,
  Still strong in chains.

"All else is gone; from those great eyes
  The soul has fled:
When faith is lost, when honor dies,
  The man is dead!

"Then pay the reverence of old days
  To his dead fame;
Walk backward, with averted gaze,
  And hide the shame!"

Ambition is not a motive power to be depended
on. If the world needed a warning, it might be
found in the first Napoleon, — a man who combined
the greatest talents with the greatest opportunities,
and who perverted both to the purposes of his
own base and selfish ambition, till all Europe had
to combine against him, and he was sent to pine
and die on a lonely island, and to spend his last
miserable days in a characteristic attempt at fal-
sifying history. Nothing so marks the intrinsic
meanness of Bonaparte as the fact that he was a
boundless liar. His baseness and his selfishness
were equalled only by his military genius.[1] He

---

[1] Even in warfare he was a barbarian. "He owed a great part
of his success to the fact that he never hesitated at any expenditure

exhausted and ruined France, and opened the way
to the equally base and selfish rule of his exceed-
ingly small and contemptible nephew and the
crew of knaves and rascals who made him their
stalking-horse. The two men will be forever gib-
beted in the pages of history as among her most
odious criminals and her most impressive warn-
ings to the people not to put their trust in any,
even the most brilliant, leaders in whom patriotism
and principle are wanting. And it seems to me to
be a good omen for the success of popular government in this country that however often in their
ignorance the American people may be deceived
by plausible demagogues, their reputation seems so
soon to collapse, no matter what may be their abilities, when once their real character is detected.

I have been reading this summer of a very different kind of politician, — a man who was brought
into political life because he was a born leader,
and who, if his life had been spared, would probably have played a great part in English history.
It was the man who in the year 1630 dared to stand
up in the British Parliament and take the lead of

of men to carry a position or obtain any other advantage ; so that
General Moreau was wont to call him 'a conqueror at the rate of
ten thousand men per hour.' " (Molinari, L'Évolution politique,
p. 289, *note.*)

those who were risking all they held dear in a determined attempt to curb the despotic tyranny of the Stuart king. When Charles threw these leaders into prison, the most sought escape by retracting and asking forgiveness; and this man might have done so too, and by what seemed a slight concession might have regained his liberty and been apparently restored to his place again. But he very well knew that to make such a concession would have been to give up the whole cause of freedom, and that though by it he would have been outwardly restored to his place, his whole power would have gone from him. Not a word would he retract. "He was still in the prime of life," says the latest and best historian of these times, "only thirty-eight years of age, when liberty is sweet. But, like Luther at Worms, it was not in him to do otherwise than he did. A word of submission would have set him free to revisit his Cornish home and the dear ones it contained. That word he would not speak."[1] He stayed in prison, and slowly died of the hardships inflicted by the pitiless malignity of Charles; and Charles, by leaving him there to perish, signed, though he did not know it, his own death-warrant. The scaffold in front of

---

[1] Gardiner, vii. 120.

the banqueting-house at Whitehall began to rise when Sir John Eliot died in the Tower; and the liberties of England were saved. A gulf wide as that between heaven and hell lies between the martyr-hero of the English and the great brigand of the French Revolution.

If we had not had such men in this country we should have had no country. I do not know how far Washington was ambitious, but I have no doubt that he felt conscious of the possession of great powers, and of the pleasure of exercising them on a great and conspicuous field; but how sternly he subordinated himself and all selfish considerations to his patriotic duty, we all know. And nothing but this perfect disinterestedness gave him the patience and perseverance that were needed to overcome his gigantic difficulties; for his greatest difficulties lay not among his avowed enemies, but in selfishness, confusion, and contradiction at home. Washington was not a great genius. In point of intellectual endowment he cannot be compared with Bonaparte, and even less in point of military genius. There were men, like Hamilton, among his compatriots who were intellectually greater than he. But there was not one among them on whom the burden could have rested as it rested on him, who could have made himself the pivot on which all things turned, the rallying-point to which all men looked because of his unswerving disinterestedness, his infinite patience, his absolute patriotism and self-forgetfulness. And I submit that in the sense in which Washington was a politician we must all, each in his little sphere, be politicians too, if we are to maintain the liberty for which he fought.

We have just erected a statue here in Boston — and no statue that we can raise will add greater dignity to our city — to a man who was all his life nothing but a poor printer. I have been often in his dingy office, for I had the happiness and honor of knowing him. He was only a poor printer; but among the men of recent times the country owes to none a deeper debt. Garrison had great abilities, — powers that might have given him wealth in one direction, political office and political distinction if he had taken another. He deliberately sacrificed all such prospects to one great disinterested patriotic task. He remained poor, and toiled on through a long life simply to free his country from the devouring cancer of slavery; and no man of his generation had a nobler or a happier life. He was not a great orator, not a great writer; but yet

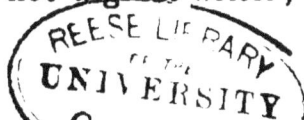

no man wielded a greater influence. Like Washington before him, he was the pivot on which a great movement turned. His power lay in those memorable words, — they have been fitly engraved on the pedestal of his statue, — " I am in earnest; I will not equivocate; I will not excuse; I will not retreat a single inch; and I will be heard." And such men when they head a great movement are always heard.

And with him was one of the greatest orators, if not the very greatest, America has yet produced, — a man born for political life because born to sway multitudes by the magic of unsurpassed eloquence. If Wendell Phillips could have paltered with his principles just far enough to open to him the doors of Congress, he would have had before him the field for the exercise of his powers which such a man must covet most. He could not palter with his principles, and those doors were forever shut. But he did not the less devote those matchless powers to an ungrateful cause, a cause in which for years he met with nothing but obloquy and abuse. With ample means for self-indulgence, he lived the simplest life. He gave all he was and all he had to what he esteemed the best and highest public objects. I think he was often mistaken,

especially in his later years. I think his objects
were often chimerical, and his aims misdirected,
for he lacked the calmness of judgment and perfect
balance of mind of his great colleague; but no
one could doubt his perfect disinterestedness.
And how infinitely small the selfish herd of political time-servers looks beside either of these men!
How petty mere personal ambition, even an honest
one, appears!

And yet I am perfectly aware that the world's
political work cannot always be carried on by saints
and heroes, and that in ordinary times honest political ambition is a good working force. There is
no more reason why a man who feels that he has a
gift for it should not enter the service of the State
than why he should not go into law or into com-
merce. There is a great deal of honest political
work to be done for the public, such as calls forth
the best talents of the ablest men. How shall such
men be appointed, and not spoilsmen and carpet-
baggers, time-servers and rogues? Here is where
our quiet man's duty comes in who does not like
politics, — a duty not to be shirked or avoided,
a duty which cannot be delegated. And for this
plain reason, — in every State there is a ruling
force, and in the long run that ruling force is the

same in every State and under every form of government.   Somewhere there is a political centre of gravity represented by the word " sovereignty," — a word we shall have to examine very closely by and bye.   Now where with us does that sovereignty avowedly reside?   Not in President or Cabinet or Congress or Legislature or Governor.   These are all merely instruments, the wheels and cranks of the political machine, not its governing force. That impelling force is public opinion.   Even under a despotism it makes itself felt; but in a republic like ours it is avowedly the ruling force, and our political machinery is constructed expressly to give it efficiency.   Now, what is public opinion?   It is your opinion and mine.   If then you and I are rascals, it is plain that like will choose like, and the community will have rogues to govern it; or if you and I are cowards, it is plain that some daring rogue will get the control of us; or if you and I are stupidly ignorant, that some cunning knave will know how to take advantage of our ignorance. Look at the stuff that is crammed down the throats of ignorant voters by political demagogues, — of whom we have had, alas! only too perfect specimens in Massachusetts.   The only parallel to political is medical quackery.   I spent some time last summer in a country village, and one day I amused myself as I waited for a purchase by examining the labels of the quack medicines which were arranged in a formidable row on the shelves of the village shopkeeper, and which bear such melancholy testimony to the practical inefficiency of our popular education. The exhibition would have been amusing if one could forget all the mischief and misery that lay behind it. Here is one label which I had the curiosity to copy: " The component parts of this remedy are Bromine, Iodine, Chlorine, Calcium, Magnesium, Iron, Sodium, and Potassium. To these we have added from the vegetable world Rumex, Dulcamara, Stillingia, Lappa, Taraxacum, and Menispermum." Imagine unlucky invalids swallowing that! Of course it was all a lie, and the contents of the bottle were probably bad rum. So the political quack's oration might be said to be bad political rum flavored with high-sounding phrases, — " money of the people," " rights of labor," " bloated bondholders," and the like, — political Taraxacum, Dulcamara, Calcium. The gaping audience does not know the meaning of the outlandish words, but think they represent profound political wisdom.

Is it not plain, then, that you and I and our quiet

friend who dislikes meddling with politics, if we are not to fall a prey to rogues and demagogues, must bestir ourselves to do our political duty; and in order that it may be done effectually, must possess political knowledge? In other words, is it not plain that the citizens of a republic must receive a sound political education, or the republic will never be safe?

What we call " law " and " government " are only the embodiment of the instincts and the will of the community as to the organization of its social relations; and it makes a great difference as to the whole course of our after speculation which of those two views we adopt which I noticed at the beginning as to what constitutes the real unit of society. If you start with the individual as the unit, the problem presents itself thus, — the state of nature is a state of perfect individual freedom; but for the sake of order and the common good the individual surrenders a portion of his native freedom to the community. The less he surrenders of this natural right to do as he pleases, the better. Government from this point of view is a necessary evil, to be reduced to the lowest terms that are compatible with the preservation of order; and that community is happiest that is governed least. The first thing to be looked after is the liberty of the individual, which before all things must be protected by a stringent Bill of Rights.

This is the famous doctrine of the social contract, which implicitly or avowedly underlies a great part' of the political writing of the last century, — the doctrine of sober John Locke in England, the doctrine with which Rousseau in France set the European world on fire, the doctrine which Jefferson borrowed from Rousseau [1] and embodied in our Declaration of Independence. It is the view which is necessarily uppermost in times of revolution, when the pressing problem of the day is to free men from bondage to a government that has proved false to its duties, and grown rotten and corrupt. But in such times there is danger of carrying this so-called democratic doctrine a great deal too far, and to confound emancipation from tyranny and corruption, which is a legitimate object, with freedom from legitimate restraint. The cure for this false view is the doctrine that is superseding the social-contract philosophy, which

[1] The doctrine is much older than Rousseau in France, or Hobbes and Locke in England; it was the doctrine of Epicurus. See Prof. Wallace's capital little book on Epicureanism, p. 158.

was but an artificial theory at best, — the evolutionary doctrine; namely, which begins with the
principle that the individual is not the unit of
political discussion, but some form, however simple,
of social organization; in other words, that man,
as Aristotle said long ago, is by nature a social
creature.[1]

Rousseau's noble savage proves to be anything
but the ideal of manhood and the model of all
independence, but rather the greatest of slaves, —
the slave of his tribe, of his king, of his priest; the
slave of superstition, the slave of his own unbridled
lusts and passions. It is not by greater freedom,
but by more and more complicated organization
that he is emancipated from all this tyranny. Will
it turn out that the individual is freest who is gov-

---

[1] In the "Politics" Aristotle not only contrasts law with compact, but seems everywhere to imply that the State neither came
into being by way of compact, nor is dependent on compact for its
authority. It began in the blind impulses which first formed the
household, and broadened then into wider aims, which nothing but
the State could satisfy. It glided imperceptibly into existence as
men became necessarily aware of the various needs bound up with
their nature. Men could not choose but form it, or some imperfect
substitute for it. It is as much a necessity of human existence as
food or fire. Its authority rests on the same basis as the authority
of the father, not on consent, but on the constitution of human
nature. — *W. L. Newman: The Politics of Aristotle. Introduction*,
vol. i. p. 27.

erned most, provided he is well governed? It is at least worth inquiry; for it is apparent that as society develops, more, and not less, government is necessary.

But now are we not in danger of being carried to the opposite extreme; for will not this doctrine, that the State is supreme, sanction tyranny; and is it not to emancipate the world from tyranny that patriots in all ages have fought and died? It is a very common view to take of history that it is first and foremost the story of a struggle to emancipate men from the bonds of tyrannical governments. But where did the tyrannical governments come from? Did the devil make the world, and begin with setting tyrants over it? No, God made the world; and such tyranny as there has been is but the corruption and decay of what was relatively good in the beginning. This mistaken view of history arises from our inveterate but very natural tendency to look only at the sensational parts of history. Happy, it has been said, is a nation that has no history, — as if wars and convulsions constituted history! But the only nation that has no history is a dead nation. Growth is slow and silent; it is only revolutions that make a noise. The oak grows silently for a hundred years, and then comes down with a crash in a thunder-storm; but do the crash and the thunder-storm constitute its history? No doubt the story of revolution is picturesque, and picturesque in proportion to its suddenness and violence. But revolution is violent change; and how can we understand it un-less we first understand the thing changed? To understand the French Revolution you must study carefully the organization and history of that French monarchy that was the slow growth of a thousand years, and that had once been the best form of government the condition of the French people admitted.

Now, it is of far more importance to the student of politics and history that he should understand the dull story of the rise and growth of that French monarchy than that he should know all about the precise way in which it came to the ground. It degenerated, as all things human do, and grew into an intolerable tyranny, and the time came for its destruction; but the instructive part of the story is not the story of its destruction, but the history of its growth. That gigantic and unprincipled bri-gand Bonaparte, who looms so largely in so many books, is a comparatively insignificant factor in French history. It was not he who framed the

Code Napoléon; that lying name is only one of the monuments of his baseness. The builder-up of Prussia, the patriotic statesman Von Stein whom he hated so, is a far greater character. Bonaparte was but a civilized kind of Tamerlane or Zinghis Khan. A man of very mean and low type may play the part of a great destroyer; it takes but a low kind of talent to be successful in smashing things: genius is shown in building them up. But building-up is a slow, dull, unromantic process; it deals with legislation and taxation, the regulation of trade and the promotion of education. To understand it you must rummage the statute-book, and fag over debates and documents and budget-speeches and treatises on finance and everything that is uninteresting. But it is pretty much so in all study. Your chemistry does not consist in a series of explosions and the exhibition of blue-lights; your physics is not the production of a series of startling surprises by turning the handles of brass and mahogany apparatus. The study of science is everywhere the study of the apparently dull and insignificant. But what appears insignificant to the vulgar eye, — a slight variation, a little change in the behavior of a compound or the result of an experiment, — is of deepest significance to the instructed. I cannot offer you any better entertainment in the *real* study of politics. If you would really understand them you must buckle down to dull work until the dulness becomes interesting. If you are satisfied with political fireworks, there are plenty of sensational histories; but remember that looking at fireworks is not studying science.

But in insisting, as I thus am doing, on the rights of government, that is, of society, as against individual rights, I run the risk of appearing the advocate of despotic power, and am taking the unpopular side; especially the side sure to be unpopular with young men. What becomes, you ask me, of all the glorification of our Revolutionary fathers' fighting for liberty; ought they not to have patiently submitted to King George? What becomes of the immortal doctrine of the Declaration of Independence, that all men are born free and equal? What becomes of the long Bills of Rights which our fathers, from the time of Magna Charta down to the time of the Massachusetts Constitution, have been continually drawing up? What becomes of the cause for which Hampden fought, and Sidney laid down his head on the scaffold? What is meant, in short, by "liberty"?

I answer that whatever may be meant by "liberty," one thing is plain, — that it cannot be the individual liberty of every man to do as he pleases, because wherever the advocates of freedom have been successful, their success has been immediately and of necessity followed by the reorganization of government; so that the struggle for liberty has never been a struggle between government on the one hand, and individuals on the other, but between the supporters of some old form of organization that was passing away, and those of some newer one that was supplanting it, — between, that is, two different forms of government. The hideous reigns of terror that sometimes intervene between the breaking up of the old organization and the formation of the new are illustrations of what takes place when the bonds of social order are once broken, and every man is left free to do what seems right in his own eyes. And if a society thus develops by the replacement by new and better forms of old and worn-out ones, — sometimes by slow and peaceful growth, sometimes through violent revolution, — it is very true that individual liberty is the gainer; but we must see in what sense this assertion can be made. It is not that the new political form is of necessity simpler than

the old one, leaving a larger space to individual
action, because it reserves a smaller sphere for the
activity of the social organism as a whole. On the
contrary, governments grow more complicated as
society develops, touch men's individual liberty
and restrain their individual actions on a greater
number of points; and yet, on the whole, it is
no paradox to say that the individual has more
freedom.

True freedom, therefore, is something very different from the absence of restraint; and Sir James
Stephen seems to me to be right when he says:
" Discussions about liberty are in truth discussions
about a negation. Attempts to solve the problems
of government and society by such discussions are
like attempts to discover the nature of light and
heat by inquiries into darkness and cold. The
phenomenon which requires and will repay study
is the direction and nature of the various forces,
individual and collective, which in their combina-
tion or collision with each other and with the
outer world make up human life. If we want to
know what ought to be the size and position of a
hole in a water-pipe, we must consider the nature
of water, the nature of pipes, and the objects for
which the water is wanted; but we shall learn very

little by studying the nature of holes. Their shape
is simply the shape of whatever bounds them;
their nature is merely to let the water pass; and
it seems to me that enthusiasm about them is al-
together thrown away. .... Discussions," he
adds, " about liberty are either misleading or
idle, unless we know who wants to do what, by
what restraint he is prevented from doing it, and
for what reasons it is proposed to remove that
restraint." [1]

There seems to me to be so much justice in this
view that the most enthusiastic advocate of free-
·dom can hardly refuse to accept it; and if we pro-
ceed to apply these limitations, we shall soon find
out the circumstances under which enthusiasm for
liberty is legitimate. The history of every country
presents great crises, where the highest duty of
every citizen was to fight for freedom even against
all the constituted authorities that claimed his
obedience; and it is according to the success or
failure of these revolts that a nation has grown
great and prospered, or decayed and perished.
And these great crises are so picturesque and so
full of stirring events that, as I have said before,

[1] Liberty, Equality, and Fraternity, 1st ed., p. 181. I am far
from agreeing with all the author's views.

they are very apt to draw attention away from
the duller parts of the story, and to constitute for
the superficial reader the whole of history.   Mr.
Motley's lively account of the revolt of the Nether-
lands has a hundred readers for one patient student
of the whole story, — the rise to greatness of the
Dutch people, of which that revolt was only a brilliant episode.   We read the story of the origin of
our own nation as if war with the mother-country
were the beginning and end of it; and certainly
to boys, and to readers who never get beyond the
boyish view of history, the story of marches and
battles is far more entertaining than the dull study
of legislation.   And yet after war must come legislation; after the military commander, the finan-
cier and the economist.   Liberty first; but liberty
to do what?   Why, liberty to impose new restraints
and form new governments, that is all; not the
liberty of anarchy.

Individual liberty and governmental constraint
may be compared to the centrifugal and centripetal forces that together keep the planets in their
orbits.   If the former were to act unchecked, the
particles of matter would fly asunder and the
whole solar system go to pieces; if the latter, all
the separate members would be crushed into an

immovable mass. In the same way the anarchy of unchecked individualism may be contrasted with the stagnant immobility of an unchecked despotic power that leaves no freedom to its subjects to be or to grow. The aim of all good government is to produce such an equilibrium between the two forces as will allow of the greatest individual freedom that is compatible with the most energetic action of the whole; and that energetic action of the whole can only be brought about by the severest repression of that liberty of the individual which is incompatible with the true interests of the community. It is no paradox, therefore, to say that the freest state will also be the most despotic, and that the evils of a despotism are not that it is despotic, but that its despotic power is exerted in wrong directions and for other than public aims. Who would complain of a despotic power that checked him from rushing headlong over a precipice? No one complains that government — that is, society — is too strong when its force is exercised in wise directions, that the public order is too orderly, that the community is too safe, that its highways are too well made, and its bridges never break down. The only questions that can arise are as to the limits of its proper functions. This indeed is at all times one of the capital problems of practical political science, but one which, from its very nature, admits of no final and definite solution; for the answer must vary with time, place, and circumstance, and the question gives rise to a discussion whose range is limited only by the extravagances of Communism on the one hand, and on the other by the individualism-run-mad of Thoreau, who from his shanty by Walden Pond proclaims the doctrine that "men are degraded when considered as members of a political organization." But as the wisest of English political philosophers says: "The science of constructing a commonwealth, or renovating it or reforming it, is, like every other experimental science, not to be taught *à priori*. Nor is it a short experience that can instruct us in that practical science."[1]

Accordingly, it will be found that the question of liberty is uppermost only in times of revolution; that is, in times when the existing governmental machinery has either become insufficient to do the increasing public work, or when it has broken down from age and imperfection. There always was a time when it was good enough, and the best that could be desired. The French Revolution did not

[1] Burke, Reflections on the French Revolution.

come because the old French monarchy had *always* been rotten and corrupt; on the contrary, France had grown under it into a great and powerful nation. It was the very growth of the nation that the monarchy had fostered that at last produced its overthrow; for the nation grew while the monarchy remained immovable. There was no talk of the claims of individual freedom so long as individuals had all the freedom they wanted. But institutions were not elastic; they would not yield to the increasing power of the centrifugal force, the growth of which they themselves had promoted; and so they were burst asunder, and out of their ruins a larger structure grew. And the process was one full of confusion, misunderstanding, bloodshed, and suffering; and unless it is for the purpose of detecting the new principles that are working themselves out into light and clearness, they are not the most instructive periods to study. The most profitable periods are those of peaceful progress under institutions that satisfy the wants of the people. You can apply the same principles to our Revolution. It was not till our fathers came to feel wants which could not be met by the government of England that they felt it to be oppressive. They were contented and loyal while they were small. But

when the increasing demands of a growing community were not met, and could not be met, by a
government three thousand miles away, they naturally began to long for independence. But it was
not an individual independence — which is anarchy
—that they fought for, but only a freedom to or-
ganize a new government, which in large measure
is exactly like the one they left. The difference is
that under it the centrifugal and centripetal forces
can be better adjusted, and both can have freer
play. There can be more of individual freedom,
while at the same time there is a better adjusted
governmental control.

A struggle for liberty, therefore, is always in the
hands of its true lovers, as contrasted with Anar-
chists and Nihilists, a struggle for more individual
freedom through a better organization of society;
while the Anarchist and Nihilist struggle for freedom
through the destruction of society itself. The Anarchist, driven wild, perhaps, by the tyranny of some
obsolete despotism like that of Russia, can think
only of his individual rights; the temperate lover
of freedom will be just as ardent in his hatred of
tyranny, but will think more of his individual
duties. The latter will therefore reach his aim
more surely, because he will not believe that anar-

chy is the road to better order, or that the way to real freedom is through blowing up emperors with dynamite.

It would seem, then, from all I have said, that it is a very mistaken view of political science and political history to look upon them as the mere story of a struggle between freedom and despotism, as if there were always two hostile parties on the scene, — the people on the one hand, oppressed and clamoring for their rights, and an enemy on the other, called government, whose chief function it was to oppress them. You might as well say that a steam-engine was made up of an oppressed element called steam, struggling for its freedom against an enemy called a boiler, that made a slave of it to turn a lot of wheels. The governmental structure is the boiler and engine that turn the tremendous social energy to use, which without them would be dissipated in thin air. The machine may be very rude and clumsy, so as to utilize only a fraction of the force; or it may be weak and defective, constantly breaking down and getting out of repair; or it may be antiquated, and far behind the best ideas, wanting in all newly invented improvements: but at its very worst it is better than no machine at all. Its defects are a good reason

for improving it, but it can never be so bad as not
to be better than none; and even though we should
admit that it may utterly break down, it would have
to be instantly replaced by a new one. The government of Turkey is perhaps as bad as a government can conceivably be; but the government of
Turkey itself is better than anarchy. We shall have
a far truer view of political science if we put aside
this antithesis between government and people,
and, using the language of the day, define it as the
science of social evolution. How far the word " social " is, and how far it is not, a wider term than the
word " political," we shall see by and bye; if we
choose to limit the meaning of the word " political,"
let us call political science one branch of the
science of social evolution. Taken in its widest
extent, it would embrace the study of all forms of
political organization from the earliest times and
among all the races and tribes of men, from the
rudest up to the most civilized, — a vast field, which
the sociologists of our day are very busy in culti-
vating, and about which the newest books have
accumulated a mass of extremely interesting material. Viewed in this light, it is a branch of
anthropology, or the study of the natural history
of man. But for more practical purposes the study

narrows itself greatly. Practical political science needs to trouble itself very little with any but the Aryan family of man, or with the histories of any branches even of that family save the European branches since their migration into Europe. Practical political science begins with the study of the political institutions of the Greeks and Romans as they appear in the earliest records of these peoples, and is virtually one continuous story from the laws of Solon and the Twelve Tables down to the Declaration of Independence and the last English Reform Bill,[1] — how vast and complicated a story, you had some opportunity to see last year. Now we may begin the study at either end: we may begin with the germs of all European political institutions at their very first appearance, and trace them step by step downwards through all the phases of their evolution, or we may begin with the last and most complete result, — say the United States or the British Constitution, — and examine all its complex details, without caring anything about its history or its origin. So you may begin with Watt's first rude steam-engine, and study step by step each

---

[1] See on this point Freeman's excellent lecture on the Unity of History. But see also the strictures of Bishop Stubbs, Lectures on Mediæval and Modern History, p. 83.

addition and improvement, till you come to the
latest result, whatever it may be, a Corliss or the
great machine that propels the biggest and newest
Cunarder across the ocean; and you may besides
study the innumerable varieties that have arisen
from the countless applications of the same principles to different purposes, — I say you may begin
with the rudest and simplest machine, and trace
all this historically; or you may begin at the
other end, and study the fully developed engine.
Each method has its advantages, and the best is a
mixture of both; for we can hardly understand
things as they are without some knowledge at least
of where they came from.   In political science the
historical method of study has of late taken the
place of all others.

And when, confining ourselves to Aryan and
European political institutions, we come to look at
them historically, we find that in the midst of all
the seeming confusion and infinity of detail there
is great simplicity; and as a few and the same
fundamental principles of mechanics and physics
govern equally the construction of Watt's rude
engine and its most elaborate improvement, so a
few fundamental principles are at the foundation
equally of the political organization of Homer's

Greeks or republican Romans, or our ancestors in the forests of Germany; and the United States Constitution is only an elaboration of a Greek republic, and a British parliament a development of an assembly of Teutonic warriors. To give an illustration, Mr. Freeman says: " It is shown beyond doubt in the writings of the founders of the Constitution of the United States that they had no knowledge of the real nature of the Federal Constitution of the Achaian League (between 300 and 400 B. C.). But two sets of commonwealths widely removed from one another in time and place found themselves in circumstances essentially the same. The later Federal Union was therefore cast in a shape which in several points presents a likeness to the elder one, — a likeness which is all the more striking and instructive because it was most certainly undesigned. Washington and Hamilton had only faint notions that they were doing the same work which had been done twenty ages before by Markos of Kyreneia and Aratos of Sikyôn, but they did the work all the same."[1]

I am aware that I am propounding a very old-fashioned kind of politics, — a doctrine that is quite at variance with a good deal of political specu-

[1] Comparative Politics, p. 33.

lation that is popular at the present day. That
speculation is based on the modern doctrine of
evolution which is so completely transforming the
whole study of physical science. Is there room
for the application of this doctrine to history? I
have already indicated my belief that there is. I
think that the doctrine of evolution is destined to
work as great a transformation in the study of
history as in the study of physical science, and
that it furnishes, *rightly interpreted*, a true key to
the origin of society, and a solid foundation for
a true science of politics. But the evolutionary
theory that is to do this must, in my judgment,
be very different from most of the sociological
systems of to-day, — it must be an evolutionary
theory, as I profoundly believe, that shall fully
recognize the existence of God and the free-will of
man as two of its fundamental postulates. Far
different from this are all evolutionary doctrines
that end in any kind of materialistic fatalism.
Mr. Buckle, for instance, in his famous book on
Civilization in England — though it is hard to say
what is the doctrine of so inconsistent a writer — in
theory at least is such a fatalist. There is a constant average, says Mr. Buckle, of so many suicides
in the course of a year, so many murders, so many

misdirected letters, and so on.   History is the
science of getting at these averages.   Progress
does not depend upon morality.   One generation
is about as moral as another, and moral precepts
were understood a thousand years ago just as well
as now.   All progress is intellectual, and steam-
engines and telegraphs are the great reformers.
You can see that this is the sort of evolutionary
doctrine that would naturally arise in this age of
many inventions.   No sane man will dispute their
importance; but a nation that is tempted to rely
upon steam-engines instead of statesmen will not
last long, for history teaches no lesson more im-
pressively than the perishableness of mere material
prosperity.   A great city may very easily be
changed into a howling wilderness.   The splendor
of London and Paris is not greater than was the
splendor of Babylon and Nineveh.   Old Rome, the
greatest of ancient cities, is a heap of crumbling
ruins, and Italy, that once ruled the world, became
for centuries the prey of her stronger neighbors.
I read in Bayard Taylor's travels in India the other
day a striking account of a deserted city he visited
there, — palaces and temples of most exquisite ar-
chitecture all so perfect that they might with little
labor be occupied again; but all solitary and

deserted, the haunt of the wolf and the jackal, the monuments of a grandeur that has utterly passed away. A day's bombardment of a single ironclad would lay our Boston in ruins. Whether Boston should be built up again would depend, not upon any fatalistic laws, but upon the question whether she contained *men*, — citizens like those of Athens described by Pericles in his Funeral Oration, of whom he says: "An Athenian citizen does not neglect the State because he takes care of his own household; and even those of us who are engaged in business have a fair idea of politics. We alone regard a man who takes no interest in public affairs, not as harmless, but as a useless character; and if few of us are originators, we are all sound judges of policy. The great impediment to action is, in our opinion, not discussion, but the want of that knowledge which is gained by discussion, preparatory to action."[1] Have we gained much on this ideal of a citizen of a free republic in the thirteen centuries since those words were uttered?

For, after all, — and it is with this moral that I will conclude, — it is *men* that make a State.

[1] Thucydides, Jowett's translation, vol. i. p. 119.

"What constitutes a State ?
Not high-raised battlement or labored mound,
Thick wall or moated gate;
Not cities proud, with spires and turrets crowned;
Not bays and broad-armed ports
Where, laughing at the storm, rich navies ride ;
Not starred and spangled courts
Where low-browed baseness wafts perfume to pride.
No ! men, high-minded men,
With powers as far above dull brutes endued,
In forest brake or den
As beasts excel cold rocks and brambles rude, —
Men who their duties know,
Who know their rights, and knowing dare maintain.
These constitute a State ;
And sovereign law, that State's collected will,
O'er thrones and globes elate,
Sits empress, crowning good, repressing ill."

University Press: John Wilson & Son, Cambridge.